MW01710345

THE SCOOP

THE SCOOP

A Story About The TAMM® Strategy And How It Can Successfully Build Your Brand

STEVE EICKMAN

With Adrienne Eickman & Jay Mindeman

Printed by Forum Communications Printing.

ISBN: 978-0-9900045-0-9

www.anchorwebsite.com

This book is dedicated to all of our clients here at Anchor Marketing, past, present and future. Also to my co-workers, who strive every day to ensure that there is sound strategy behind each project. Thank you all. Together, we're going to do great things.

Contents

Introduction

I used to fix transmissions.

There, I said it. I didn't get an MBA from an Ivy League school. I didn't invent a social media website and make a billion dollars. I worked as a mechanic until I got a job servicing and selling dishwashers at restaurants. Turns out I was pretty good at the sales part of that job, so I tried my hand in the radio business selling advertising. That led to a job selling advertising and writing commercials in the cable TV industry, and finally, to an account management position with a growing advertising agency.

Why did people keep offering me jobs? Because I listened carefully, then I thought strategically, then I spoke clearly. Many sales professionals skip right to the end of that list. They tell you about themselves and their company and their products, but they never really take the time to find out about you or your needs.

Listening and strategic thinking. I didn't invent these concepts, but they've somehow managed to set me apart, and they've most certainly helped my clients to succeed. For my entire career—especially when I finally started my own marketing agency—I was practicing an effective system for approaching communication that was unique in its simplicity. I just didn't realize it.

One of my hobbies is singing. I sing in the shower. I sing in church. I sing when I mow the lawn. People tell me that I'm a pretty good singer, but I don't think about singing very much; I just do it. It was the same thing with marketing. I was writing marketing plans and helping my clients to build brands with great success, but I struggled to explain exactly how I did it.

Fixing a transmission involved a proven set of steps, a process that included analysis and action that anyone could perform if they had the right tools. I just needed to think about my marketing and brand building the same way. What were the steps to properly planned communication?

A few years ago I began to record my processes, and my methods soon came into focus. It was like searching for fingerprints—they were always there,

I just hadn't seen them until I spread some dust around. The results were exciting, and I knew right away that I didn't just want to share my technique, I wanted to teach other business people how to do it themselves.

Everyone likes stories. Somehow they connect with us more than lectures. I suppose we see something of ourselves in the characters. That is certainly the case with the character of Charlie in the story you are about to read. He and I have a lot in common. We both started from humble beginnings, and we both learn by doing.

This book is my way of teaching others how to successfully plan their communication based on each unique target audience. I call it the TAMM method, and you'll find that it is a powerful way to improve your marketing, advertising and overall communication.

It's a story about listening, thinking and communicating—in that order. It's also a story about ice cream and bluegrass music and family. But I'm getting ahead of myself. Read on, and enjoy.

Chapter 1

Chapter 1

"… I'd like to know just who you've been talking to!"

Charlie stopped mid-step, his jacket still in his hand, his ears perked up at the office door. Just on the other side of that door, he knew that John, his boss, was standing, his shoulders raised up to ear level, his neck and ears red. He could tell that John's back was to the door by the way his voice was slightly muffled, but the fact that Charlie could still make out every syllable seemed to be a bad sign. Just a few moments ago, Charlie had recognized the gray BMW parked out back as belonging to Brian Burns, the owner of The Scoop Ice Cream Shoppe.

Okay, he corrected himself, *a very bad sign.*

He started up again on his path to the staff lockers and hung up his jacket. Then he turned around, rubbing his hands together, and waited. He glanced at the clock again, feeling uneasy. If he waited too much longer, the shop wouldn't be ready to be opened by 10. But then again … he hesitated, and even as he hesitated, he became irritated with himself. Charlie had always been a hesitater, waiting for someone to tell him what to do, rather than taking charge himself. And he'd known John for 30 years—and John was the exact opposite. He was the very definition of a 'take-charge' kind of guy.

Charlie ran a hand through his hair and then took a few steps toward the dishwasher. He could get out the scoops and start taking the lids off the buckets. He could do that much without waiting for permission to get started.

Out front now, he waited to hear the office door open and close. He waited to hear John's footsteps going quickly out the back door, where he would chain-smoke a few cigarettes, and then his returning footsteps—slower, easier and calmer. Brian might come out and say hello, see how Charlie was doing, but maybe not, and the day would get started.

But instead all he heard was muffled voices from the office.

His eyes flitted up to the clock. 9:50.

The bell on the front door jingled, followed by a soft thud. He looked up to see June, his "co-worker." He always mentally put quotations around this title when applied to June, as she liked to play it fast and loose with the term "work."

The soft thud was her backpack hitting the ground. As Charlie looked up, June was lazily taking her earbuds out of her ears and winding them down into the pocket of her hooded sweatshirt. She motioned with her chin toward the back. "Beemer." She said bluntly. It wasn't a question and really wasn't much of a statement, either. That's how it was with June.

"Morning, June," Charlie said, and he smiled a little. Maybe it was because he had two daughters at home only a little younger than June, but he was developing a little bit of a soft spot for his blue-haired, black-and-white-striped-legging-wearing "co-worker."

She looked at him for a minute, her dark eyes passing through him like he was made of water, and then turned and went out of the shop, reaching for her cigarettes as she went.

Okay, Charlie thought, *maybe I only like her because I don't know her very well.*

He nervously went about the shop, taking down chairs and wiping counters. Really, at this point, he was just keeping his hands busy in case Brian and John came out of their meeting. He didn't want to be standing there idle if they did.

10:06. Charlie flicked the red OPEN sign on by the door and waited, noting inwardly that June was nowhere to be seen. He parked himself uneasily behind the cash register and resumed his natural state: waiting.

Suddenly, the office door slammed open as if it had been pulled off its hinges. Charlie straightened up with a start, taking a few steps toward the back, and then retreated, wondering if he really wanted to get himself in the middle of whatever was going on.

"You can be expecting legal recourse! At the very least!" John was bellowing. Charlie couldn't see him but could imagine him with his mind's eye clear as day: purple-faced, hands shaking, lips white and eyes becoming narrower and narrower by the second. This always seemed to happen when Brian stopped in for a visit, and it seemed to be happening more and more these days whether or not Brian was there. Charlie didn't know John as well as he used to, but he knew that things weren't going great at home.

And they certainly weren't going well at the shop, either. Charlie knew that the numbers lately had been bad and were getting worse. John was spending more and more time in the office, leaving Charlie in charge out front. Charlie did the best he could—but it seemed like he didn't really have the magic touch when it came to getting people to do what he wanted them to do.

" ... And good luck finding someone else to run this silly operation you've got going here—yeah, good luck! When I walk out that door, I am gone, do you hear me?"

Charlie wondered why he was asking, as Brian was sitting only a few feet away. Charlie was pretty sure that people across town could hear John at this point. Charlie was annoyed but not surprised. This was pretty typical—this was when John threatened to quit, and Brian begged him to stay. Then there would be some chain-smoking and a quiet morning, and everything would go back to normal until the next visit.

"John," Brian said quietly. "I am asking you to leave my property. Right now."

Charlie was sure that he had imagined it. He took a few steps toward the office, just to be sure that he wasn't hearing things. Had John just been fired?

The front door jingled, and Charlie spun on his heel, expecting to see June. Instead he saw two boys, about 12 years old, grinning and racing each other for the front. In the parking lot, a woman who was most undoubtedly their mother leaned against her van, looking harassed. One boy clenched a bill in his fist and plunked it down as he reached the counter.

"Well, howdy," Charlie said, "what's the scoop?"

The boys ordered their ice cream, and Charlie

scooped it up carefully, mixed in their toppings ("Gummy bears! And sprinkles! And those thingys—what do you call those? Cookie crumbles!"), and handed them each spoons and napkins. The boys spun around and made a run for the door, leaving their napkins behind.

"Keep the change!" one of them yelled, and Charlie dutifully placed the change—a few coins—in the large pickle jar labeled "Support Counter Intelligence."

Then he heard the back door slam and turned around to see Brian standing behind him.

"Ah, yes. Charlie," Brian said. He was a small man, trim—especially for someone who owned a chain of ice cream shops. But old. Brian was standing perfectly still, his shoulders slumped and heavy, as though he were holding a heavy toolbox in each hand.

" 'lo, Brian," Charlie said, trying to sneak a glance around him to see if John was somewhere in the back.

"Yes, ah, well. Is June here yet? I'd like to speak with you in the office."

Charlie cast his eyes quickly around the parking lot and spotted the top of June's blue head by the dumpsters.

"Yeah—she's just—uh—hold on. I'll grab her."

Charlie reached the front door in a few steps

and put two fingers in his mouth—and then reminded himself he was calling a "co-worker," not his daughters. Sighing, he walked through the parking lot and to the dumpsters.

"June," he said, in what he hoped was a firm voice. "June, something's happened. Brian needs us back in the shop."

"John just drove off," she said, motioning again by jutting her chin. "Where's he going?"

"I don't know," Charlie replied, feeling his irritation rise. "But I think Brian wants to tell us. Let's go back to the store."

She turned back to look at him as if her eyes were burning laser beam holes into his face.

"I'll be there in a minute!" she snapped as she put her cigarette out on the ground.

Charlie went back to the shop, taking long strides. Facing his boss again, he said, "She'll be right here."

Brian nodded slowly, as if in a daze, and went back to the office. He left the door open.

Charlie heard the struggles, coughs and snuffles that usually announced the dramatic return of June. He waited as she made her noisy way over to the counter and took up her post behind the cash register. She reached for her phone before he'd even made it around the corner, and he wondered ruefully if teenagers ever had a single moment of private, quiet reflection.

"Brian?" he said, knocking with his knuckle on the open door. Brian was sitting in the office chair, looking at a blank computer screen. There was something else behind him that was new—a screen that was on, full of tiny video screens. *Security cameras*, Charlie thought. He could see June, texting away on her phone as a customer made their way to the counter.

"What's the scoop?" June said tonelessly behind them as her figure on the screen made no move whatsoever.

"Come on in, Charlie," Brian said. He reached for the doorknob to close it behind him. As he sat down, Brian clicked the monitor behind them off. Charlie was glad—he wasn't sure he'd be able to have a conversation while watching June's terrible customer service going on just a few feet away.

"As you see," Brian began, and Charlie snapped back to attention. "I've installed security cameras. Several—nine in total. They are all over the store, in the back, in the parking lot and in the front. I'm sure you realize why."

Charlie didn't know anything specific—John had never shared anything like that with him—but he knew that there was only one reason that a business that had never had security cameras before would suddenly install nine of them. He nodded and said slowly, “Someone been stealing?”

“Yes—for months,” Brian answered. “Maybe longer, but I only began noticing recently. As you can imagine, this is quite a shock to me. I’ve never dealt with anything like this before. I had the cameras installed a few months ago—you remember we were closed for a few days … ”

“Oh,” said Charlie, “Yeah, I do remember—but I wasn’t working here yet.”

“Oh, I see,” said Brian heavily. “Of course.”

For a moment, he just looked at Charlie. Charlie had the distinct impression of being sized up.

“Well,” Brian rushed on, “this way I could keep tabs.” He stopped suddenly, leaving something unsaid.

“Okay,” Charlie replied, when he felt the silence had stretched on long enough. What did this have to do with him?

“Well—so—here’s the situation,” Brian began again. “After some surveillance … and um … data collection, I suppose you would call it, John has been let go. He won’t be coming back.” Charlie felt like he’d been punched in the stomach. He and John weren’t exactly friends, but still, Charlie couldn’t believe that John would have been stealing from the shop he’d been managing for years.

"As you know, summer is our busiest season, with the resorters and people traveling through … " Brian was saying, "I can start a search for a new general manager, but things like this take time. Most people who want jobs over the summer have them already; this is such a small town you've got here … "

Charlie nodded along, still not understanding why he was having this meeting. June wasn't going to want to hear any of this from him—if she wanted to hear it at all. As for their night guys—Kenny and Cohen—they were probably already hearing about it from John. The four of them—John, June, Kenny and Cohen—had worked together for awhile and were very close. John was a well-liked boss, giving an infinite number of smoke breaks and second chances. The odd man out had been Charlie, who had only started working at the shop a few months ago—and only as a last resort, and only because his wife demanded he find something to do outside the house after he'd lost his job at the paper mill.

He shuddered inwardly thinking about it—he hated the term "lost his job." He didn't *lose* it—he hadn't done anything wrong, other than not seeing the writing on the wall soon enough to find himself another job before it'd been too late. And then the mill had closed down after a year of layoffs, and Charlie had found himself with hat in hand.

"I guess what I'm trying to say," Brian said, which brought Charlie back to the present. "Is that there isn't really anyone else to help me out here. I can start a search, but that could take time—months, maybe, after the busy season. I've got new stores opening all across the state. And here I've got a store full of teenagers and … "

"And me," Charlie said, the reason for this conversation suddenly dawning on him.

"Exactly," Brian replied. "And you."

Brian leaned forward and said, "Charlie, I need you to take the reins here. At least for now. At least for awhile. I need to be out of town getting those other stores open—I really don't have anyone else that I can plug in here. After the summer is over, we can have a conversation about our next step."

Charlie said nothing. Taking orders was his thing—it's what he was good at—but this order seemed like too much.

Brian was nodding his head and rubbing his hands together again. Abruptly, he stood and reached for the door. Charlie guessed that meant the meeting was over and stood with him, and they walked out into the front.

June was sitting on the counter, cross-legged,

playing with her phone. When she saw the two men coming out of the office, she hopped down and grabbed a washcloth, taking a halfhearted swipe at the counter.

"June, Charlie can fill you in on all the details, but John is done at this store," Brian said. June's eyebrows shot dangerously high on her forehead, and she turned her dark gaze back to Charlie.

Details? What details? Charlie thought. June probably knew more about it than he did.

June stared with her mouth set in a hard line. She looked over at Charlie and then said, "So, is he in charge now? Or what?"

Brian clapped a hand on Charlie's shoulder and said, "He absolutely is."

Chapter 2

Charlie leaned against the sink in his kitchen and sighed. He closed his eyes and let his forehead relax. His wrinkles were becoming so etched and deep that soon he was sure they would start developing wrinkles of their own.

"Hey." A voice behind him spoke, and Charlie heard the swing of the kitchen door as his wife came in behind him. She walked over to the fridge and opened it, rooting around for the ice cream in the back of the freezer. Charlie watched her, wondering how someone so tiny could possibly eat so much ice cream. He also wondered, with a jolt, why they were buying so much ice cream from the grocery store when he was the manager of an ice cream shop.

"Hey," he started softly, "do you think maybe we could start buying ice cream from the shop? Instead of the store."

"Sure," Andrea replied airily. "But they don't have the kinds that the girls like, and it also only comes in one huge size, so if you're willing to fight over which girl gets to choose the flavor, be my guest."

"Okay, okay," he replied, knowing she was right but hating the lecture. She could have just said no.

She moved beside him and leaned against the counter with the dish rack. "What, no comeback? What's the problem tonight?"

Charlie hung the dishtowel on the faucet and said, "What else? Work." Andrea nodded and made a face that he knew was meant to be commiserating, but he wasn't sure if Andrea had ever had a bad day at work.

"Do you want to talk about it?" Andrea asked him, and Charlie knew this was routine. She always asked if he wanted to talk about it, and he always said no. Because Andrea had a million things on her mind—she ran the bank in town, and she ran the household—Charlie hated burdening her with his problems, especially when they were problems that had nothing to do with her and that she couldn't solve.

But a thought struck him, and he stopped for a minute to think—Andrea ran the bank in town and had been doing it for years. She was a nice woman, sure, but there must have been some employee, at some point, that didn't like the job. A worker who just wouldn't *work*.

And even if she was just gifted with extraordinary business sense and talent—she also kept both their girls in line—a feat that even after 15 years Charlie could not accomplish. He dreaded nights when Andrea was gone and he would be left to sort out the girls' schedule and routines. Now that they were older, Charlie found himself just staying out of it.

And doing what I'm told, he thought and shook his head. There was no one at the shop to tell him what to do anymore. And everyone seemed to know it.

His day at the shop had gone from bad to horrible so quickly that Charlie still wasn't sure what happened. When he arrived, the dishes weren't all the way done from the night before. Almost, but not quite—a few scoops were left by the front counter, a few spoons in the sink. He stared down at the floor and saw streaks from the mop—and wasn't sure if he should just be glad that they at least *attempted* to mop or upset that they did such a lousy job. He had glanced at the clock and sighed heavily, wondering how much time he had to catch up from the night before, perform all the opening duties and then *somehow* get to the mountain of paperwork waiting for him in the office. He knew without even thinking about it that there was no way he could get June to do the extra work. She probably wouldn't be there early enough to get it done in any case.

So he had mopped, done the dishes and opened the store. Then he had waited on the first few customers, and by the time June got there, he was red in the face. She stared at him, emotionless, while he asked her why she was late.

"It's ten after. That's not late," she said. "Talk to me about thirty minutes, not ten."

"Okay, June," he said, "but I have a lot to do. I need you here on time."

"Right, right," she had said, reaching for her phone. "Well, I can't change the past, so. That's it, boss."

She had looked down at her phone, her thumbs flying. Charlie was furious—but didn't know what to do. She knew she was late. She didn't care. She was here now, and he could finally get to the impending avalanche of papers in the office.

He had spent the entire morning and most of the afternoon sorting out all the papers. Charlie had no questions about John's ability to manage the shop, but apparently during the last few months he had started to let things slide. As far as he could tell, the shop didn't owe anyone money, but he couldn't figure out when the last time an inventory had taken place. It had been awhile since they had ordered things like paper products, disposable bowls and soap for the bathrooms.

There were also things around the shop that had

been bothering Charlie since he had started working there—things that only someone who had spent years working on an assembly line would notice—like how inefficiently the back of the shop was designed, so that buckets of ice cream were often left next to a hot dishwasher while they waited to be put in the counter, or how the scoops were stored such that they dripped onto the floor all day long, creating a gummy, sticky mess at the end of the day. On his first full day as the general manager of The Scoop Ice Cream Shoppe, Charlie was pretty grateful that he was only going to be the manager for a few months.

Eventually, Kenny and Cohen came in to replace June. Charlie had gone out to discuss with them the need to close the store properly. Cohen had stared down at his shoes the whole time, and Kenny had just stared at him with a small smirk on his face. Charlie found himself demonstrating how to use a mop at one point, and realized while he was doing it that they obviously knew how to use a mop—they had always closed the store just fine for John. He had awkwardly put the mop down and then said, "Just do it. I don't want to do your jobs and my job at the same time."

"O-kay," Kenny had said finally, and he and Cohen had both walked away. Within minutes, they were behind the counter laughing. Charlie couldn't be sure, but he thought he saw Kenny imitating him with the mop.

At the end of the day, Charlie had gone home exhausted, much more exhausted than he had ever been, even after a long day at the paper mill. Now he sat here, staring at his wife and wondering how she had been able to manage so many employees all these years, working her way up to a top position at the bank. *Some people just have "it,"* Charlie thought jealously.

Andrea put her hand on his arm and asked him again, "Do you want to talk about it?"

"It's just … " Charlie tried to think of a way to say it without sounding totally pitiful. He decided just to go for it:

"How do you get people to do what you say?"

Andrea blinked at his point-blank question.

"Forget it," Charlie said instantly, turning back to the sink, embarrassed and frustrated. He was a grown man, after all, and the father of two girls—how could he not know how to get people to listen to him?

"I think," he continued, "I think I'm going to have to fire everyone and hire new people. I know that the girls said they wanted jobs this summer—I could hire both of them and maybe one of their friends?"

Andrea shook her head softly, staring at him like she'd never seen him before.

"Michelle and Kara do want summer jobs, and would probably work at the shop with you. But you can't just fire a whole crew and then hire your daughters to replace them—especially in a small town."

Her eyes suddenly looked distant, and she moved across the room quickly to a drawer where they kept odds and ends. Charlie had seen this before—she often would get sudden inspiration and need to jot down an idea. *Hopefully,* Charlie thought ruefully, *this is an idea that involves her coming in and firing my staff for me.* He was suddenly filled with a new, terrifying thought—what if he fired everyone and they just came back the next day, refusing to let him fire them?

Andrea was sketching something on a piece of paper. Then she looked up at him, smiled and said, "Now, don't laugh."

Charlie raised his shoulders to his ears and let them fall. He had absolutely no idea what he had to potentially laugh about. Andrea motioned him over to the table, and he sat down. He was staring at a piece of paper with four shapes, letters and arrows drawn on it.

"TAMM," he read aloud and then looked up at Andrea, who was looking a little sheepish. "Maybe

I should ask *you* to promise not to laugh. What is this? Are you jerking me around?"

She did laugh—but it wasn't a mean laugh. She threw up her hands. "You asked how I get people to do what I say—this is how I do it. I'm laughing because all of my girlfriends will think I'm crazy telling my husband how I get him to do what I ask."

He looked back down at the letters, shapes and arrows. "What?" he said finally. "You have a … a process? A method for getting me to do what you want?" He looked back up at her, and she was watching him with merriment in her eyes. He realized she had misunderstood.

"Honey," he said gently, motioning to her drawing. "This isn't what I meant. I didn't mean you—or the girls. I mean at work."

"Oh, I know," she nodded and sat down next to him. "You remember when I had that internship in college on Wall Street? My mentor taught me this, 20 years ago. He used it all the time—I would watch him talk to people and could tell he was using TAMM—it kind of became an inside joke between us. After awhile, when I got more comfortable, I started using it, too. And then … you know, a long time later … " She looked at him guiltily, "I started using it at home, kind of by accident. But it worked—and so it kind of became habit. Now I use TAMM all the time, basically whenever I need someone to do something." Seeing his incredulous look, she tapped the piece of paper with her pencil and said, "TAMM. Target, action, message, media."

Charlie stared at his wife. "You're telling me … you're telling me that for the last 18 years you've been manipulating me somehow? Some kind of … what, mind game?"

She laughed again. "No, no, nothing like that," she said. "It's not manipulation—you aren't lying, you aren't being deceitful. You're simply … " She paused for a moment, looking for the right way to say what she was thinking. "You're simply *planning your communication*."

Charlie was dumbfounded. He'd never felt so in the dark when talking to Andrea. She was grinning broadly, and he found himself grinning back.

"Okay," he said. "I'll bite. Now what on God's green earth are you talking about?"

Chapter 3

Chapter 3

"Charlie! Charlie!" June's shrill voice brought Charlie out of the office as if being drawn by a magnet. He had never heard her voice have any amount of energy before, and had never heard her use his actual name.

"June? What's going on?"

She was standing by the cooler, holding a bucket of ice cream. Mutely, she pointed at the floor. Charlie looked down to see about the worst thing the manager of an ice cream shop could see.

"Aw no," he said, shifting his weight and balling up a fist. "Melting … "

There were different colors of ice cream all over the floor of the freezer, just starting to run down to the floor. He realized then that he couldn't hear the regular hum of the freezer—it was off. *Must have been off for quite some time to get those huge buckets to melt.*

"All right, June," he said. "Go ahead and finish opening the shop." To his surprise, June scurried off toward the front of the shop to do the rest of the opening procedures. *I didn't even have to use TAMM,* Charlie thought, and then realized that June was probably just happy that she didn't have to be the one to clean up this mess.

Charlie did all the usual things with a freezer—he checked the "on" switch. He checked that it was plugged in and then checked to be sure that there was power in that outlet. Very quickly, he had exhausted his short list of things that he knew how to fix. He realized that June was standing on the edge of the dining room, watching him.

"Hey, June," he said finally. "Do you think … ?"

She continued to stare at him warily, unmoving. He quickly changed tactics, remembering what Andrea had said the night before:

"TAMM—the T stands for TARGET. You have to think about who you are talking to. You can't talk to everyone the same way—think about it."

"Sure I can!" Charlie had balked. *"They're employees—they're my employees! I treat them all the same!"*

"Of course—if you're talking about pay rates and how many breaks they get," Andrea had answered. *"I'm not talking about treatment. I'm talking about* communication. *It just doesn't make*

any sense to talk to a 19-year-old girl the same way you talk to a 50-year-old man."

They had talked for a long time about June—discussing her as a target.

"She's young—and she's broke," Andrea said flatly. *"Unlike Kenny and Cohen, she is paying her own bills and renting her own place. Your ice cream shop is her steady job, but it isn't her only job."*

"She's a musician ... " Charlie remembered. *"She does nights and weekends playing her guitar around town."*

"Right," Andrea agreed. *"She has blue hair, she is never dressed the way she is supposed to be, she has a permanent chip on her shoulder, she's young, and as far as you've ever heard, she doesn't have anyone else helping her. So ... what does that tell you about her?"*

"She's independent," Charlie said, the answer coming to him clearly. *"It's not that she doesn't want to work, she just doesn't want to work for us. She wants to do her own thing."*

"Good," Andrea said. *"I'll give you one more hint, since you're new at this. There's only one reason that someone is chronically late. She is absolutely determined that whatever it is that she's got going on is more important than the ice cream shop—and she wants you to know it. She doesn't*

want to depend on the shop. But she likes it that you depend on her—and the only way she knows that you depend on her ... "

"Is when I holler at her for being late," Charlie finished, shaking his head at the complexity of people's minds.

"So, as far as a target goes," Andrea said, motioning at the paper where she'd been scribbling notes, *"You need to talk to June in a way that makes her feel what?"*

"Creative and independent," Charlie said right away, thinking of June's blue hair and music. *"And a way that makes her feel like the shop really needs her."*

"There you go," Andrea had said and put the cap back on her marker with gusto.

Charlie gathered his wits about him and reminded himself—she's creative ... independent ... and wants to feel like we depend on her.

Charlie took a deep breath and began again:

"Hey, June," he said, and she jumped slightly. He hoped his voice sounded cheerful and a little playful. "You know how I used to work at the mill?" He glanced up at her, to see that she was staring at him with wide eyes.

"Well, I did," he continued as he reached for the mop and the bucket. "I didn't have a very important job—but I figured, you know, while I was there, I might as well get good at it. So I showed up every day and did my little piece of the puzzle, and after so many years I started to like it a little bit." She was chewing her gum slowly … but still listening.

"When my girls were born—you know I have twin daughters?—well anyway, when they were born, I had to take some time off because my wife, Andrea, was in the hospital. When I got back to the mill, there were all these people telling me that I could never take time off again, because I'd gotten so good at my job that no one else could remember how to do it without me." The mop bucket was full of hot, steaming, soapy water. He put the mop in the water and then stood to face June.

"So they gave me a raise."

The gum bubble that June had been blowing popped. Her eyes narrowed suspiciously.

"What are you trying to say?" she asked.

"Well, I was just thinking … " he said, "I was looking over the staff files, and it looks like you haven't had a raise in a long time."

"Are you giving me a raise?" she asked, and for the first time, Charlie saw a little bit of light flick in her eyes.

"No," he said, and she deflated instantly. "The

point of my story was: I didn't really like my job. But I did like getting a paycheck. So I made myself indispensable to my boss—and THEN I got rewarded. That's what I need from you. And then we can talk about a raise."

"I don't know how I can get any better at this job," she replied, a little bit of a whine in her voice. "I serve ice cream. I clean up. That's it."

The little edge of desperation in her voice was enough for Charlie to know he had her. Exhilarated with his success, he handed her the mop and said, "Come on, June. You're a smart, creative girl. We're counting on you."

He walked back to the office and closed the door. Then, unable to help himself, he turned to look at the security monitor.

June stood there staring at the mop for a few moments. Then she sighed heavily, wrung out the excess water and got to work.

Charlie stared in disbelief—he got her to do something! But that nagging voice in the back of his head disagreed. *That wasn't using TAMM. That was using money as a motivator. Use money as a motivator for anyone and it will work.*

He remembered what Andrea had told him, *"Think of how you talk to Michelle and Kara. You could offer Michelle a million dollars to clean her room, and she would still only do a haphazard job. We have to find other ways to get her to clean up."*

"Sure—like threats!" Charlie had joked, but on reflecting, he realized that wasn't true. As a young girl, Michelle had needed challenges and games—like seeing how much she could clean in 20 minutes or telling her to pick up all the blue blocks before Charlie could pick up all the red blocks.

Kara was the exact opposite. She was a born negotiator. Sticker charts, rewards and eventually allowance were her main motivators for doing chores.

"And praise!" Andrea had reminded him. *"That's a message all in its own!"*

He looked again at the screen and saw that June had finished mopping and was now considering the freezer. She looked around, as if seeing if anyone was watching, and then got down on her hands and knees and started to scrub the corners and the door of the freezer—a job that Charlie wasn't sure had been done since he'd been there.

He sighed, thanking his lucky stars that the plan was working, and then turned to the computer to find the number for the freezer guy. His next round of communication was about to begin.

Chapter 4

"Nope, sorry man. Can't do it."

Charlie couldn't believe it. He passed a hand over his eyes and looked up at the clock—10:30. The shop was open, with all the ice cream buckets up front. In just ten hours the shop would close, with nowhere to put the ice cream overnight. And the repair man was telling him he couldn't be there that day—and was only a *maybe* for tomorrow.

"Okay," Charlie heard himself saying. He was already trying to think about what he would do—take all the ice cream home with him? See if June had a freezer big enough for two of the huge buckets? He stared at the computer and considered searching the Internet for a repair video and hoping he didn't botch it.

He suddenly thought about his discussion with Andrea the night before—and the second part of the TAMM strategy—*action.* He needed this tech to come and fix his freezer; that was the action needed here. Immediately. This was a problem that was out of his hands—he needed this technician to do it.

He considered how the phone call had been going so far—after finally being connected to the technician out for repairs that day, the tech told him that he was totally booked up for the day, and that there was no way he could possibly help. Charlie had been awkwardly pleading with him, recognizing that a small note of desperation was creeping into his voice, but the technician had held firm: he was too busy today. He'd have to find a way to get through until tomorrow night. Because the freezer was under warranty, they could only go through this contracted company for repairs or the warranty would be void.

The phone call ended, and Charlie sat looking at the post-it note that he had posted that morning with the four letters that Andrea had drilled him on the night before: TAMM.

Well, a fat lot of good that did me, he thought angrily, considering ripping the note down and tossing it in the trash. Then a memory from the night before came back to him, and he heard his wife's voice as if she was there in the room with him:

"You're focusing on the action. You need to figure out your target first."

Charlie stopped and sat back down. On the

monitors he watched June serve a few customers ice cream, reaching around the extra buckets that were propped in the cooler to keep them frozen.

Okay—so, a target. What kind of guy was the technician?

Charlie sighed and furrowed his brow. He'd never met this technician. When he'd been practicing with Andrea they had targeted June, Cohen, Kenny and his daughters. They hadn't talked about how to plan communication with someone you didn't know.

He sat down at the desk and turned over the billing statement. Absentmindedly, he drew a stick figure drawing of a technician. And then he wrote:

TARGET

He gave his stick figure a hat and a tool belt. And then he sat, considering. He wrote the words "male" and the name of the company he worked for. He knew from dealing with this company in the past that their technicians often had some HVAC training post-high school and that they were all drug-tested. He wrote those things down as well.

And then he pondered. What was the key here? What else did he know?

Then he wrote:

BUSY

At the bottom of his paper, he wrote the word:

ACTION

And underneath it, he wrote: "I need him to fix my freezer." But just as he was finishing this sentence, he realized that wasn't really true. The action he needed was that the freezer got fixed—as long as it ended up working again by the end of the day and as long as he didn't call another company to fix it, did it really matter if this specific technician was the one who did it?

He altered his sentence to read: "I need my freezer fixed."

Feeling energized, he picked up his phone and punched the numbers to the technician's mobile phone. When he answered, Charlie introduced himself again and then said,

"I'm sorry about earlier. I'm real stressed about this freezer, as I'm sure you can imagine. Now, you said that you are booked up with service calls all day, is that still correct?"

"Yes, sir, as I said—" the tech began, and Charlie cut him off—knowing he was pressing his luck, but he just didn't want the tech to hang up.

"Sure, sure—I totally understand. So what I'm wondering is—do you think you could maybe do some work with me, over the phone? Maybe while you're driving to your next stop, you could kind of walk me through it?"

He was met with silence from the other end, and Charlie waited, realizing he was holding his breath a little.

"Well … " the tech began, "I don't know if that's really legal—I mean, that means I'm kinda doing the work for free, right?"

"You can still bill me for the time, of course." Charlie replied. "Your supervisor will think you're a genius—all that time spent on the road, and you found a way to make money doing it!"

The tech cleared his throat and then said, "I don't know if I can tell you how to fix it—but I suppose we can do some troubleshooting. What kind of tools do you have on hand?"

Charlie balled his hand up into a fist and punched the air as a tingle of warm pride spread down his spine. The freezer was getting fixed. He had done it!

"Let me run out to my truck," he heard himself saying. "What will I need?"

Chapter 5

"How was work?" Andrea asked him airily on her way through the kitchen. Once again, they were performing their nightly rituals: Andrea was clearing the table, and Charlie was doing the dishes. After 18 years of marriage, it felt good to have these routines in place … but Charlie liked this new development as well: his wife asking him about his job and him being able to share with her something substantial.

He caught her up with his use of the TAMM strategy that day, and how well it had gone with June and the repair tech—who was able to troubleshoot a problem with a wire and tell Charlie how to get it running for the next few days until he could get there to fix it. Charlie felt like he was walking on air.

Andrea was impressed with how he had used the TAMM strategy on the repair tech—"It can be hard to adapt to a situation like that," she said—but was a little less impressed with how he had dealt with June.

"It's not that it wasn't good!" she insisted. "You got her to do some work and that was the action you wanted, right? It's just … I feel like you didn't really need to tell her your whole life story."

"What?" Charlie said. "I was just trying to relate to her a little bit, let her know that I know where she's coming from."

"Sure, hon," Andrea said. "But does that really align with your plan? I mean, it worked, so I can't complain too much—but I think you might have stopped focusing on your target." Charlie shrugged his shoulders. Andrea went on: "The message you delivered to her is this: 'Impress me, and you will be rewarded.' Or, put another way, 'Work hard, and I will give you a raise.' Right?"

"Okay … " Charlie said, agreeing.

"Okay. So you told her a story about yourself and wrapped your message up in it. You spent what, three minutes of face time delivering that message?"

"Yeah … " Charlie said slowly, not understanding where Andrea was going.

"Think about your target. June is 19, a musician, chronically late and has a crazy wild appearance. Do you know what that says to me? Self-involved, self-involved, self-involved. She doesn't care about your stories; she doesn't need to hear them to convince her of anything. In fact, I'm shocked she went for it. It would have made more sense for her to say, 'Who cares what you used to do at the mill

20 years ago? This is me and this is now.' It would have made more sense, honestly, to just straight up tell her succinctly: 'Work hard, and I will give you a raise.' Or, if that felt too awkward, you should have told her a story about herself, a time that she impressed you and how she should keep it up."

Charlie was totally flabbergasted. "See, this is manipulation!" he declared, "because I can't think of a single time that June has impressed me! What am I supposed to do—lie?"

Andrea laughed and reassured him, "It's not as big of a deal as you are making it out to be. She did the work; she got the message and took action. So there you go. You're new at this, you're learning. You've just got to think about your message." She flipped her hair over her shoulder and stared off into space, and then continued, "Do you remember when I got promoted to front end manager? Maybe 15 years ago?"

"Sure," Charlie replied. They were expecting the girls at the time, and the bump in pay had been needed.

"Well, right after that happened, I almost lost my job. For exactly this reason: I lost track of the target." Charlie searched his mind but couldn't remember this story. He leaned forward in his seat to indicate to Andrea that she should go on.

"Well," she began and told him about how the

bank was coming out with Internet banking at the time. Everyone at the bank was really excited about it—"So excited," Andrea said, "That we forgot about our target. We got consumed with our message—Internet banking is here!" Andrea told him how the management team got together to work on marketing for the product launch, and then finally the day came.

"And?" Charlie prompted.

"And it was a huge disaster!" Andrea said, chuckling a little. "We had gotten so wrapped up in our message—we wanted everyone to create an online profile, a username and password, and so we created our plan based on getting this information out. We completely lost sight of our targets—we're a small bank in a small town. Probably 75 percent of our customers at the time were senior citizens who'd been banking with us since they were teenagers—and here we were asking for them to set up a password to access their accounts from computers they didn't even own. We wanted their account information, their social security numbers, et cetera." Andrea rolled her eyes at her past self. "Looking back on it now, I cannot believe that it didn't turn out worse than it did. As it was, we realized after the first month of the launch that our customers weren't happy—so we had to backpedal a little."

"But … " Charlie said. "But surely you didn't axe Internet banking? You'd be way behind the industry if you had!"

"Exactly—think back to TAMM," Andrea said, sitting up straight and getting back into boss-lady mode. "Our Action hadn't changed—we wanted people to sign up for Internet banking. Our Target hadn't changed, either—we just had to refocus. We were so wrapped up in our message that we—a group of thirty-something executives—didn't realize that we had written a message for a target that didn't exist."

"You're losing me," Charlie said. "So how did you get them to sign up for Internet banking?"

"Did you take any journalism in high school?" Andrea asked Charlie, which seemed like a huge change of subject. Besides which—he thought ruefully—Andrea knew full well that Charlie's electives had been full of shop classes, sports and the occasional art class—certainly no extra writing.

"Well," Andrea breezed on, writing down a few words on the paper in front of them, "have you ever thought about how they write headlines?"

All the time, Charlie thought sarcastically. "Not really," he told his wife.

"Well, there are some studies about words and their power on people. For example, look at this:"

She showed him the paper, upon which she had written the words,

CAR CRASH

Charlie stared at them, and then looked back up at Andrea expectantly. "Okay?" he prompted.

"Describe to me what you're thinking," she said.

"Car crash … " Charlie mused, feeling silly, but realizing that Andrea hadn't steered him wrong so far. "Well, I guess in my head I am picturing cars smashed and mangled—maybe several cars. Maybe police sirens in the background and some terrible circumstances—like ice or rain or it's dark."

"Okay, good," Andrea said, and then turned the paper over. "Now what do you see?" she asked, showing him another message:

CAR COLLISION

Charlie was shocked as the image in his head changed. "A fender bender," he said incredulously. "Two cars, maximum. Broad daylight, no injuries."

"No big deal, right?" Andrea said. "And yet, the two words mean basically the same thing. But they conjure up two totally different images in your mind." Charlie nodded. Andrea took the paper away and said, "This is important Charlie—because this is something that everyone struggles with. When you consider your message, *every single word pulls some weight*."

As if to emphasize her point, she sat back in her chair and gave him a moment to consider. Then she launched back into her story about Internet banking.

"So, we changed our message. We started to focus on being a small-town bank. We pointed out other things that we had done in the community—other ways that we had been pioneers—over the 100 years we've been in business. We tried to plant the idea of Internet banking in our customer's minds as just one more step in a natural progression of innovations. We realized that the things we'd been talking about—like speeding up transactions and eliminating a lot of the tasks that the drive-through tellers performed—were messages targeted at us. Our customers could care less about those things—what they wanted to hear about was security, trust and how this would improve their control and efficiency with their funds. We started focusing on the customer and how Internet banking would be good *for them*."

Charlie sat and thought about this and his interactions with his colleagues—no, his employees—at the shop. He thought about the time he'd been talking to Kenny and Cohen about proper closing procedures, and how he had launched into a long discussion about responsibility and pride in one's work.

That would have worked for me, he realized with a jolt. He had been spending all his time thinking about how to get his employees to work harder, but all the messages he'd been delivering were ones that would have worked for *him*—they had nothing, really, to do with those kids, his targets.

"Okay," he said slowly, "so let's go over this again. The first thing I do is analyze my target."

"Yes," Andrea agreed. "So important that you understand who you'll be talking to."

"Okay. And the next thing I do is analyze what action I want them to take, even though that seems pretty obvious."

"Careful!" Andrea cautioned. "Think about the repair tech you talked to, and how you realized you had the wrong action in mind. You didn't need *him* to fix the freezer, you just needed it fixed somehow. You'd be amazed how easy it is to really dig into something and then realize it's the wrong action."

"And then I worry about the message—as it pertains to the target and the action."

"Right. Good job!" Andrea said, not at all trying to patronize. Despite himself, Charlie felt a smile growing across his face.

"Okay … so, next we have to talk about media," Andrea said, with a smile on her face. "And I'm excited about this—because this is going to open up whole new levels of communication for you." She grinned a little mischievously and reached into her purse—ominously pulling out a cellular phone.

"What's that for?" Charlie asked, as Andrea thumbed it open and handed it to him.

"Charlie—I'm going to teach you how to send a text message," she said, and Charlie laughed.

Chapter 6

"Uh … Charlie?" June's voice spoke behind him. Charlie was sitting in the office, looking over his massive to-do list. At the top of that list was ordering paper supplies and confirming a shipment of ice cream. Somewhere on the list was also discussing closing procedures—again—with Kenny and Cohen.

Out of habit, Charlie looked at the security monitor and saw a man standing in the store by the register with no ice cream in his hand. He looked pleasant enough, so he didn't seem to be a disgruntled customer. Charlie wheeled around and looked inquiringly at June.

"Uh, some guy is here for you. I guess he's from the newspaper? He says he wants to talk to you … ?"

Charlie's eyebrows shot up, and he looked around June.

"Seriously?" he said. "What for?"

In answer, June stepped back from the door and motioned with her hand at the front of the shop and then disappeared around the corner. Charlie stood up and ran a hand through his hair and then laughed a little bit at himself. He and June were about the two most ill-equipped people to deal with this kind of situation. He thought fleetingly of calling Brian, or even Andrea, and then shook his head. Charlie took a deep breath and then walked out, pasting what he hoped to be a confident smile on his face.

"Hey there, I'm Charlie Givens," he said. "What's the scoop?"

"Howdy!" the man replied with vigor. He stretched his hand out to Charlie and said, "Jake O'Reilly. And I hope you realize the irony of asking a newspaper man what the scoop is."

"I'm aware," Charlie replied, although he hadn't thought of it until the man said something. *So much for planned communication*, he thought.

"Well, I'm here to talk to you about The Two Inlets Festival."

Charlie was a bit of a hunter, as a hobby. He had often stared down the crosshairs of his rifle at a deer who suspected that he'd been targeted. And Charlie was sure that was how his face looked at this moment.

"The Two Inlets Festival?" Charlie repeated. "The bluegrass concert?"

"Yes," the reporter said, recognizing some confusion on Charlie's end. "Well, it's in two weeks, and the newspaper likes to do a special section that profiles the sponsors—"

Sponsors? Charlie had time to think the question, but not to voice it, because there was a stifled cough from behind him. He turned to see June standing by the door, a broom in her hand.

"Charlie, can I talk to you for just a second?"

"I—June, hold on," Charlie said, turning back to the reporter.

"I'm really sorry," June said, with a nervous note in her voice. "I need to interrupt *right now*, just for a second. It's urgent."

Thinking of the newly repaired freezer, Charlie turned back to the reporter and said, "I'm so sorry—I'll be right back."

He hurried back to the freezer, asking as he went, "Is this darn thing out again?"

"No—it's the festival." Charlie stopped and squinted at June.

"What?"

"The festival—John signed up to do the festival because I asked him to."

"What? June, what are you talking about?"

"The Two Inlets Festival! I asked John if the store could be a sponsor because I want to go."

For a moment, Charlie didn't even know what to think. It was like his brain had become a cloudy void. He couldn't even ask June to repeat what she had just said, because none of it made any sense.

"June," he said quietly, aware of the reporter standing only a few feet away, "that is absurd." He hoped he wasn't hurting her feelings, but he also knew that there was no way that John would have done something like this without telling anyone. But then the most absurd thing of all happened.

"I know," June agreed, and her eyes looked remorseful and embarrassed. Charlie thought he could see red appearing across her pale face. She looked like she might cry. Charlie reminded himself that John and June had been very close and that June was an aspiring musician. For the first time, Charlie analyzed John as a target. He was middle-aged but surrounded himself with young people that were subordinate to him. Charlie had always known John to be a successful businessman, but in the last few years something must have changed. He was recently divorced, and his grown children lived far away. He liked to feel important and needed. Charlie changed his mind. Agreeing to sponsor the festival so that June could go was exactly the kind of thing that John would do.

"It's guaranteed all-access admission for

sponsors," June grumbled, and Charlie sensed a little bit more of her usual defiance coming back to the surface. "Three days of admission, plus a campsite, plus access to the bands—"

"I know, I know," Charlie stopped her. The price of regular admission to the festival for all three days was prohibitive for a lot of people; in fact, most of the local townsfolk didn't attend. But people traveled from all over the country to attend the bluegrass festival, big names and small. It made perfect sense that June would want to go. But still— "June, when were you going to tell me about this?"

"I don't know," June said. "I just didn't want you to say I couldn't go."

Charlie ran a hand through his hair—he was sure it would be standing straight up by now—and sighed, realizing that if the newspaper had sent a reporter, there was probably no backing out of it now in any case. "All right, June," he said. "We'll talk about it later."

He walked back out to the front and greeted Jake again, apologizing, and then said,

"Okay—so about this profile. What can I tell you?"

An hour later, Charlie sat again in front of his to-do list. Only now he had added, in huge red letters, TWO INLETS MUSIC FESTIVAL.

He considered the phrase heavily, and, as if a bad taste were forming in his mouth, he wrote these words under them: MORE HELP. He sat back suddenly in his chair and put his hands behind his head. He thought through his next few steps. The festival was three days long, from midmorning to midnight. The ice cream stand wouldn't need to be open the whole time … *But it should be.* Charlie thought wryly. He picked up a pencil and absently tapped it against the desk.

Okay, he thought, deciding to just accept what was to happen next. The festival would need to be staffed by two, maybe three workers—and one of those workers would need to be June. The store in town would also need to be open, and with the influx of tourists that the festival brought in, it might even need to be more staffed than usual.

Charlie pulled up to the desk and brought up the word processor on his computer. He typed the words: HELP WANTED. Then he typed the following words: "Four or five temporary workers needed at The Scoop Ice Cream Shoppe. Apply in person at 225 Circle Hills Drive, Monday through Friday, 10-5. Ask for Charlie."

Then he used the Internet to find out how to

submit a classified ad to the newspaper and copied his text into an email. Then he stopped, on second thought, and decided he'd better run it past Andrea. He'd never done anything like this before, and she did it all the time.

He typed a quick email to her explaining the situation and then clicked send. He sat back down to look over his order form, realizing he was going to have to increase his order to cover the festival and was almost startled when his cell phone rang. It was Andrea.

"Are you forgetting everything we've been talking about?" Andrea asked, getting right to the point.

"What?" he asked, incredulous. "I need some temp workers for the festival—so I wrote an ad. My target is the people looking for work, the action I want them to take is to come apply for a job, I sent you my message, and the media is the newspaper."

"So, yes, basically, you are forgetting everything we've talked about!" Andrea replied. "Let's start with media—we just talked about this last night! Tell me about why you chose the newspaper."

"Well," Charlie started, "the newspaper is where people go to look for jobs. The other media we talked about—like a phone call, or a text message, or a face-to-face conversation, none of those will work for this kind of target."

"Okay," Andrea said, "you're right about those media not being correct for your target—and let's talk about the target here. Your target is people looking for jobs."

"Yes," Charlie agreed.

"Anyone looking for a job?" she prompted. Charlie was about to repeat himself when he paused. This smelled like a trick question.

"Well … yeah, I guess."

"So … old people? Grandmothers? College students? People with business degrees? Doctors? Lawyers? Out of work IRS agents?"

"Okay, okay," Charlie cut her off. "Why don't you get to the point?"

"You are looking for temporary workers that have a specific skill set—for example—you need people that can be on their feet for a long time, do some physical work quickly, can work a cash register and don't mind not getting paid a ton. Oh, and it would be helpful if they could sell some ice cream, right?"

"Um, sure, I guess," Charlie agreed.

"OK, then you need to write an ad that is going to get THOSE people to apply. Especially since Brian has been running the ad looking for a new general manager—running these together might be really confusing."

"Huh?" Charlie said, suddenly confused, and then he remembered. *That's right ... I won't have to do this forever. Just for a little while longer.* Charlie was surprised to find that the fact somehow made him a little sad.

"Okay—so you're going to work on your message based on this new target, right?" Andrea asked him.

"Oh—yes, absolutely," Charlie said, coming back to the conversation. "Anything else?"

"Yes, Charlie—and really this is why I called—you have to think about the media you're using. Do you remember what we talked about last night?"

Charlie stared at the monitor blankly, trying to figure out what she wanted him to say.

"Media is how you choose to deliver your message," he recited from their conversation the night before. "It has to be geared toward your target as well."

"Exactly," Andrea said. Charlie remembered their discussion from the night before, when Andrea had taught him about all the different ways the word "media" was used. "*What most people think of is the news—journalism,*" *she had said.* "*That's exactly how we're using the word, too—they use newspapers, TV, magazines, whatever—to deliver a message. And the medium that they choose depends on the message. For example, you aren't going to see an emergency weather announcement in a newspaper. And you aren't going to see the local high school football scores being reported on the national news."*

There were other ways to think of the word "media"—but they all kind of meant the same thing. *"For example,"* Andrea had said, *"artists often choose what medium to specialize in. Some use sculptures, some paints, some write poems. It all depends on how they feel their message needs to be carried. And there are spiritual mediums,"* she said, smiling a little, *"who say that they are receiving a message and delivering it. That's all we're talking about here—looking at our message and deciding what's the best way to get it to the right people: our target."*

"Now, when you think about what we just said was your actual target for these positions—well, what kind of people do you think they are?"

Charlie floundered. As usual, he didn't know what she was looking for here.

"Well, you know—what you said," he sputtered. "People who can scoop ice cream and run a cash register and work long hours." He stopped to think about it. "And who don't get paid much, and who—well—I guess young people."

"Good," Andrea agreed. "Young people. Now I want you to think about this festival—what kind of people do you want to be representing your shop in front of the thousands of people who might have never had an experience with The Scoop before?"

Charlie froze. Suddenly the whole thing seemed ridiculous. "Andrea," he said, a little impatiently. "You're making this into a big deal and it isn't. I just need two or three extra hands—"

"Honey," Andrea interrupted, "I'm sorry, but it *is* a big deal. John left the shop in a big mess. Sales are down, your employees are less than stellar, and this is your first big test as a general manager. What is it if it isn't a big deal?" When Charlie said nothing, Andrea rushed on, "Charlie, business is all about taking the sweet with the sour. This festival is happening whether or not you wanted it to, so you might as well take it as an opportunity to develop The Scoop. Once you've figured out what kind of people you want working for you, you need to figure out how to get them to apply and the best way to tell those people about it. Those *specific* people, Charlie, not just anyone."

"Okay, Andrea," Charlie said, heaving a great sigh. "I'll get on it."

"Good," Andrea said. "Call me after you decide."

She hung up, and Charlie realized—not for the first time—how Andrea had quickly risen to the top of her company.

He started to think about what they had said about the target for the want ad. Young people, who were strong and able to stay on their feet for a long time. Someone who could run a cash register and didn't need to get paid a lot. He chuckled a little bit—sounded like him when he was in high school. If only he could show up at football practice and pass out job applications.

He paused in his thoughts. Something was bothering him, something that Andrea had said. He went back over their conversation in his head.

"Oh, and it would be helpful if they could sell some ice cream, right?"

He had never thought of what they did at the shop as "sales." People wanted ice cream, they came in and bought it. But he supposed that at a festival, with so many people and so much competing business, it would take more than just a hankering for ice cream to make it worth his time being there. Being a sponsor would help, sure, but still. Even though Charlie had been a good football player, he had never been extroverted enough to make a good salesman.

No, Charlie mused, football players wouldn't work for this. For this kind of a job, he needed … well, he needed …

"Cheerleaders," he said aloud. His eyes rested on a photo on the wall of his two daughters at a basketball game. Michelle was wearing a jersey, strong, proud and a little haughty—and next to her was Kara. Holding pom-poms, smiling brightly, proud of her purple and white uniform.

He sat back down at the keyboard and tried to think about what kind of an ad would get Kara interested in working the festival.

He wrote:

"Who doesn't love music and ice cream? The Scoop Ice Cream Shoppe is looking for outgoing, friendly people to work at the Two Inlets Music Festival. Workers will enjoy all-access passes for the entire festival, competitive hourly wage and ... "

"And what?" Charlie asked himself. What motivates teenagers?

"Work with your friends, enjoy the festival—and keep it cool with a few scoops!"

He shook his head at himself. His old mill buddies would be laughing right now.

Feeling a little exhausted, he copied the words into an email for Andrea and then typed the word: MEDIA.

And stared at it.

"Think of a circuit," Andrea had said to him. *"You have a power source on one end and a lightbulb on the other. Media is how you carry the current from the power source to the lightbulb. Some things will work and some things won't, and some just won't work as well. You need different wires, different switches and different setups for different jobs."*

Andrea was right about his ad, Charlie knew. He had never seen Kara or Michelle open a newspaper. They were way too busy staring endlessly at their cell phones.

Cell phones, Charlie thought. He wished that there was a way to get a text message simultaneously delivered to every teenager in town. Thinking of that made him think about the job website he had cruised after the mill closed. He wrote down the word: INTERNET.

Okay, so he could put out an Internet ad. But he felt like there needed to be something else—some other way to hit his target. What else would his girls notice?

With a jolt, followed by dread and apprehension, Charlie remembered the only other thing teenagers cared about as much as their phones: their cars.

He looked at the monitor and sighed. Then opened

the door and called for June. She came quickly—a change from usual—and Charlie smiled and tried to sound positive as he told her about hiring a few temp workers for the festival and how he wanted some young, friendly, outgoing people to help out.

"So, I need to get this help wanted ad to them as quickly as possible," he went on. "I'm going to post it online, too, but I thought there might be an even faster way … " He laid out the details of her mission and then waited for the protest to begin.

June stared at him, her blue hair looking even bluer as her face turned red. But she didn't object.

"Okay," she said. "So you want these on the cars of all the teenage girls in town? Basically?"

"Well," Charlie said, "that would be ideal."

"All right. When you've got them ready, I'll take them to the mall and put them on all the cars that have something sparkly or fuzzy in them," June said wryly, and Charlie found himself smiling.

"Thanks, June," he told her. She turned to walk away, then stopped and came back.

"Charlie? Where are you going to post the ad online?"

"Uh," Charlie thought for a moment, and then told her the name of the website he had used to look for work after the mill closed. But even as he said it, he knew that wasn't right. *You're not the target!* he reminded himself.

June came toward him, pulling out her phone. She thumbed through a few screens and then said, "I was just thinking—you know about social media, right?"

Charlie nodded. His daughters were obsessed with sharing, liking, commenting and posting about every single moment of every day of each and every one of their friends and enemies.

"Okay, well, you know that might be a faster way to get around to everyone, right? And probably way cheaper. Use this site." She showed him a profile that had been set up for The Scoop, which Charlie had never seen before. It had very little content—but a lot of followers.

"How do we have so many followers?" Charlie asked. "I didn't even know about this."

"Times have changed, old man," June said, but not meanly. "Whenever kids go anywhere they instantly check to see if it's on these sites—to see if there are coupons, deals, what everyone else is ordering there, whatever. So John made profiles for us on a few of the bigger social media sites, but I don't think he ever used them."

Charlie stared at June's phone. Even though Andrea had taught him how to text message the night before, looking at this site felt like staring at a spaceship. He handed it back to June.

"Okay—" he said. "Can you put this on there?"

He showed her the ad. June looked over the text and then, thumbs flying, typed it into her phone. She showed it to him again and said, "Done. That's it. All our followers are getting that notice right now on their cell phones."

"June," he said, genuinely impressed. "Thank you."

He might have imagined it, but Charlie was pretty sure he saw her smile as she walked out.

He sent the email to Andrea and then called her cell phone. She answered on the third ring and said,

"Hold on, I'm reading it right now."

After praising him for his changes, she got right back to business. "Okay—I like your message, so now how are you going to deliver it?"

Charlie explained to her how he was going to put fliers on all the teenagers' cars at the mall. Andrea laughed.

"A little old-fashioned," she said. "But not totally unreasonable. Kind of like a direct mail campaign."

"And one other medium," Charlie said and explained what June had done. Andrea was thrilled.

"Charlie, that's brilliant!" she said. "And I think you're right on track with your target—in fact—we should talk to Kara and Michelle tonight and see if they want to help out. Now get back to work—the festival is coming up!"

Charlie hung up the phone and felt a weird, warm feeling in his belly. He realized that he was starting to kind of like this whole manager gig.

Chapter 7

Chapter 7

Charlie stared at the phone as it rang, a bad feeling in his stomach.

He had just come back from a run to the store, and a note was taped to the office door.

"Brian called," it said, in Kenny's messy scrawl. "He'll call back."

He sighed, reminding himself that it could mean anything or nothing and picked up the phone.

"Good afternoon!" he said. "What's the scoop?"

"Charlie, it's Brian."

"Well hey there, Brian, I was meaning to call … "

"Yeah, I would assume so—but instead I have a picture of my shop in the newspaper talking about sponsoring a music festival? Did you approve this?"

Ah ha, Charlie thought, *someone who reads a newspaper* ... He shook his head to clear his thoughts and said, "Ah, well, sort of. The festival sponsorship, I guess, was John's idea. The newspaper man showed up and wanted to do a story about us so I kinda went with it."

"And when were you going to tell me about it?"

"Well … " The honest answer was that Charlie had completely forgotten that he should inform his boss. He was still so used to John doing all the communicating with Brian. "I'm sorry about that, Brian, it's just that we've been so busy, and I guess it just slipped my mind."

"Busy? Busy with what?" Brian asked. Charlie wondered where to start.

"With getting ready," he said simply, thinking of the order forms that still needed to go out, the batch of applications he needed to go through and the signs he needed to order.

"All right, Charlie—but I should have been told. The shop is in a major transition right now, and we certainly don't need extra stress."

"I agree," Charlie said, and he meant it. "But I couldn't see a good way to wiggle out of it just then, so I decided to roll with the punches."

"All right," Brian said. There was some quiet on the phone, and Charlie wondered if they'd been disconnected.

"All right, Charlie," Brian began again. "I've been searching for a replacement for John all summer, and I've had a few inquiries. After the festival is concluded, you and I can sit down and go over the new applicants. I'd like your opinion on who might work well on the team."

"Sure," Charlie said, but he had that sinking feeling again. They ended the call with the promise that Charlie would be more forthcoming in the future, and Brian said he would be coming to town for the festival.

Charlie hung up the phone and closed his eyes. He tried to picture the festival. Two Inlets was a lot like most music festivals, in that there were performers from all over the country, food and drink vendors, and a massive crowd—but it was more than that. Two Inlets was artsy—hoity-toity, as Charlie's daughters would say. The crowd wouldn't be made up of your weekend concertgoer—these were well-to-do, educated people that were really into bluegrass music. They flocked to the little town every year for the festival; it was a huge money-maker for the bed & breakfasts and resorts in town. *And the restaurants,* Charlie mused.

Suddenly his eyes flew open. He realized what he'd just been doing—sizing up the festival attendants like they were targets. Thinking of the action he wanted them to take—he wanted them to buy ice cream—made him realize that he could use TAMM to help him with this.

He sat up to the desk and got out a new piece of

paper. He wrote down his target—the festival guests—and the action he wanted them to take. *Buy ice cream,* he thought ruefully. Pretty cut and dry.

He thought back about everything he knew about advertising and marketing—which wasn't much—and how Andrea was always telling him to think deeper, that there was more to things than just face value. So he considered—in an ideal situation, he would sell a lot of ice cream, but could there be more? He wanted all his customers to leave happy—so he wrote that down, too. *Buy ice cream and have a good experience.* The next idea came to him suddenly, and he realized it was a bit of a game changer. He added: "Tell their friends."

Then he pondered his message—how could he get them to have this great experience and tell their friends about it? What could be said to a customer to make them more likely to choose his ice cream over someone else's?

A memory surfaced of Andrea, so many years ago, feverishly cleaning their house while they waited for their pastor to come over to meet the twins, who were newborn babies. Charlie was trying to get her to sit down, promising her that the pastor was not going to care about whether or not the baseboards were clean.

Andrea had looked at him tiredly. She smiled

and said, "It's a touchpoint, Charlie. I can't stop with my *touchpoints*."

A touchpoint, she had explained, was kind of like a first impression. "But to be more accurate, you would need to call it a *total* impression. All the little glimpses and moments with us form an impression of who we are: the way we dress, the things we have around our house—and yes, Charlie, whether or not our baseboards are clean." To illustrate her point, she showed him the trash can in the nursery—full of diapers, wipes, Kleenexes and empty bottles of lotion, diaper cream and formula cans. "Imagine you are an archaeologist," Andrea had suggested. "It's a thousand years from now, and you come upon this trash can in a dig. What assumptions could you make about the people using these trash cans, based solely on the contents?"

Well, Charlie remembered thinking, he could assume a lot. That the trash can belonged in a nursery or at least a house with babies. That the parents either never took the trash out (not true) or there were a lot of babies (true, or at least it felt that way at the time).

"This is a touchpoint, Charlie," Andrea had said. "This says something about us—about the kind of people we are."

Charlie wondered why that had come up just now and then realized that Andrea had talked to him about it another time, when the bank lobby was being remodeled. One of the big discussions for her had been the direction that the customer traffic would flow, to control noise, privacy and efficiency. But they didn't just change the layout of the building—they changed the way that customers were treated by bank personnel. For example, when they came in for any sort of appointment, they were to be greeted at the door and escorted to the appropriate office or desk and offered something to drink. Bankers were given 15-minute time slots between appointments to review files and refresh their memories—so that when a longtime customer came in, the banker could greet them by name and would know a few things from their banking history.

Andrea didn't know if any of that extra time led *directly* to more business, but she told Charlie that she knew that it couldn't hurt—and as years went on there were more and more instances of people using the bank because a friend or family member had recommended it.

"In an unsure economy," Andrea had told him over dinner one evening, *"if you can't offer better prices or interest rates, you have to offer better service. The experience of working with us has to be*

better than with anyone else, otherwise you can't be sure if the consumer will choose you or not. It will all be guesswork and random chance."

Okay, Charlie thought, released from his memories to his present-day office, *if I can't offer better prices or a better selection than the other ice cream places, I need to think about my touchpoints and build an experience for the customers.*

He looked back to his paper, and next to the word "Message" he wrote: "We provide a great experience, and we also provide great ice cream."

Then he crossed it out, remembering what Andrea had told him about every word carrying meaning. He wrote with a strong hand: "We are the best ice cream experience."

There, he thought, knowing Andrea would approve. Then he wrote down the word MEDIA, and for once it was clear to him that this was a message that would not work in newspaper, fliers or via the Internet. This was a message best delivered face-to-face. So he wrote down: "Word of mouth."

And then he turned to the pile of applications, determined to find a handful of ice cream ambassadors that could help him deliver the message.

At the end of his day, Charlie felt wiped out,

but satisfied. That morning he had chosen seven applicants that he liked (including his daughter, Kara) and was able to get them all in for interviews that afternoon. He had hired four of them—and even remembered to keep in mind that he needed to hire people that could both deliver his message *and* work well with June, who would be working the festival all three days.

He was currently just tidying up his office, moving applications to the shredder, when his hand grazed a bunch of papers clipped together underneath the phone. His brows furrowed—he thought that he'd picked up all the applications. It was the order form for supplies, the one that he had been putting off all week because he wasn't sure what to think about the festival. The one that was due that day by five o'clock.

His eyes flitted up to the clock—and saw that it was ten after. He practically dove at the phone and tore the receiver off the hook, dialing frantically. It was agonizing to wait until the phone was answered.

Charlie identified himself quickly and then asked if he could read off his order, since he hadn't submitted it online. There was a pause.

"I'm really sorry, Charlie," said Becky, the agent at their supplier. "But orders have to be submitted online by five. It's after five there—which means it's after six here. The trucks are getting loaded up right now."

"I know, I know," Charlie said. "But I really need this order—in fact, I need an extra order—we have a festival here this weekend … "

"Charlie, I wish I could help, but there's really nothing I can do."

Charlie paused for a moment, thinking fast. Automatically, he started sizing Becky up as a target. He had never met her before but had talked to her a few times over the phone. He knew that she was a veteran in the company and that she was a very good employee. Their supplier sent out periodic emails, and Becky was mentioned several times for different achievements. Charlie felt like he was stomping sloppily through a mud puddle in his brain, grasping for anything that could help him.

The agents weren't paid on commission, so promising her a huge order wouldn't persuade her to help. They were under contract with this supplier, so threatening not to use them next time wouldn't work, nor could he just call a different supplier.

But that thought gave him a pause.

I don't need the right message for this one, he thought, *I need the right target.*

"All right, Becky, you win," he said. "Thanks much, I'll talk to you next week or so."

He disconnected quickly and grabbed John's rolodex. He sifted through it quickly until he found the number for Scott Johnson, the consultant that worked for the supplier. Scott's job was to drive the truck that brought them the ice cream, unload it and help them work out their order for next time. Things had gotten confused when John left and so they'd missed the last consultation with Scott.

But, Charlie remembered, *Scott works on commission.*

While he dialed the phone and waited for Scott to answer, Charlie thought about his strategy. Under ordinary circumstances, Scott would love having a large order. Scott benefited directly from having a large order, and the potential for having larger orders in the future would convince him immediately that he should do whatever it took to get the ice cream there in time.

Getting him to agree to the late order wouldn't be the action that Charlie needed Scott to take. What Charlie needed Scott to do was something that Charlie couldn't do himself—persuade Becky.

"Hello? Hello?" Lost in his thoughts, Charlie hadn't noticed when Scott had picked up.

"Hey there, Scott, it's Charlie Givens." Scott's

tone warmed up immediately, and Charlie wondered if Scott had already noticed that he was missing their order, which would be hurting his bottom line. "You probably have noticed that I haven't put in my order today."

"Well yeah, Charlie, I was seeing that—you know I probably should have given you an extra reminder call earlier this week."

"That would have been great, Scott, but I probably would have forgotten anyway." He outlined what the store had been going through to get ready for the festival—laying it on extra thick that there was going to be a need for lots—and lots—of ice cream.

"Well, let me take a look here, Charlie," Scott said, and Charlie could hear papers being shuffled. "I think what would be easiest here is to repeat your last order, but triple it. That way we've already got everything inputted in our system, we just have to resubmit. But there's one problem."

Charlie said, "Yeah I know—it's after five. I just got off the phone with Becky, she won't take the order. I was hoping you could persuade her."

"Well, that's going to be a bit difficult," Scott said, "Because my route has been set already—if I deviate from it then I have to pay the mileage. Of course—if *you'd* be willing to pay the mileage, then I'd be happy to throw your ice cream on the back of my truck, and you can leave Becky to me."

Charlie stopped for a second, considering. It occurred to him that maybe Scott had some training in TAMM himself.

"All right, Scott." he said. "You've got yourself a deal. When should I be expecting you?"

After working out a few details with Scott, Charlie walked out to the front of the shop to find Kenny with their new hires—Kara and three others, two girls and one boy. After they had been hired that morning, Charlie had asked them to come back that evening for some training. The festival was just a few days away, but Charlie was finally starting to feel optimistic. Things were looking up.

"How are we doing?" he asked June quietly.

She looked up and said in a gloomy voice, "You wanted cheerleaders. Well, here ya go. Good luck, Charlie. I'll see you tomorrow." Charlie smiled and then addressed the group.

He ran over a few obvious tips—such as the company greeting ("What's the scoop?") and how to scoop the ice cream into an attractive cone. He had copies of the shop's menu to hand out to them, asking them to learn it as well as they could by tomorrow, when he would have them working behind the counter with June. They were going to be rotating who was working at the store and who would be working at the festival.

He was trying to keep his tone light, excited and upbeat. His targets were a group of kids who were outgoing, fun and ambitious. During their interviews they had all made excellent eye contact, talked easily and had genuine smiles. They all were good students and participated in extra-curricular activities, which Charlie hoped could mean that they were smart and responsible.

The action he wanted them to take was to sell ice cream, but also to create a culture. He wanted to be known for being an ice cream *experience*, not just an ice cream shop.

So he explained to them how he wanted repeat customers—"And not just repeat customers—I want every customer to become a repeat customer. You're not just selling ice cream, you're selling the experience. You're selling the great time that you and your friends are having."

So, there. He had laid out the action that he wanted them to take. He had delivered the message in such a way that he was pretty sure they would go for it—except for this.

"At the end of each day, whoever sold the most ice cream gets a hundred dollars, cash in hand," he said and then let it sink in. He saw exchanged looks, smiles growing and shoulders straightening. "Three days means three hundred dollars—on top of your hourly wage—if you are the top salesperson each day. Our ice cream is good—it's delicious—but at the end of the day, what's going to make them come back for more is not the ice cream. It's you."

Charlie took out a marker to write on a large piece of paper he had taped to the window.

"Now, let's talk about how we can accomplish that," he said. He wrote the letters T A M M down the side of the paper.

"The T stands for Target," he told them and he drew an arrow pointing to the T. "Right now, we're going to call the Target the festival audience—but that's pretty general. When it comes down to it you're going to want to address each audience member as their own specific target. So, tell me. What do we know about the people at the festival, in general?"

After a few moments of quiet, the teenagers started shouting out answers—and most of them were pretty good.

"All right, all right. The next thing we need to figure out is the Action we want them to take. So—what do you guys think?"

"Buy ice cream," one teenager said. "Obviously."

"Buy *a lot* of ice cream," another suggested. "And come back again the next day."

"And bring their friends," Kara said. Charlie felt himself swelling with pride as the other teenagers looked at her. "What?" she said. "When you love something you tell people about it, and they want it too. That's how it works."

Good girl, Charlie thought and wrote, "Bring their friends" next to the other actions they had already discussed.

"The first M stands for Message. And this can be tricky. Our message is whatever it takes to get the target to do what we want them to." He pointed back at the T and A in his chart and then waited for their ideas.

After a few minutes, the boy spoke up. "Do you mean, like, a literal message? Like something that we are actually going to say to them? Or do you mean the entire picture—like what you were saying earlier, the experience?"

"You're exactly right!" Charlie said and wrote 'experience' by the M. "We call them touchpoints. Your touchpoints are everything that a person sees, senses or experiences around you. And the sum total of all of those things creates an impression for the viewer—so while the words you're saying in your message are definitely the message, you have to be mindful of your touchpoints, because ultimately they can be just as important. You could be in the best ice cream shop in the world, but if you noticed that your server had dirty fingernails, what are you likely to tell your friends?"

The teenagers were nodding at each other, all except Kara, who was smiling a little bit and had a faraway look in her eyes. Charlie wondered if Andrea had already taught Kara all about touchpoints.

"The other word you can use for it is 'culture,'" Charlie said as he wrote it down. "Culture means a lot of things, but it's similar to touchpoints. The culture at a football game is different than the culture at a ballet recital. The culture at a church is different than the culture at a restaurant. We're an ice cream shop—so our culture is already one that's about fun, indulgence and relaxing. What else can we do to build a culture that makes people come back?"

"Be friendly," one girl said immediately. Charlie wrote it down by the M.

"More than friendly," the boy countered. "We have to be like—you know. Kind of act like we're already friends."

"Can you give me an example?" Charlie asked.

"You know," the boy said, "like instead of saying, 'Thanks, have a good day' at the end of the sale, say, 'Okay, see you tomorrow.'"

Everyone turned to look at him. Charlie was more than impressed. He glanced down at his notes. “Doug, right?” he said. The boy nodded, and Charlie said, “That’s a great, great idea. Tell me another one.”

“Okay,” Doug said and smiled. “Well, if you’re already friends, really good friends, and you’re throwing some kind of like … a birthday party, you might say something like, ‘Hey, where’s your girlfriend? Don’t you think she wants some ice cream too?’ We could say that to the customers—you know—kind of plant the idea in their head that it might be nice if they had brought their buddies with them.” Doug spoke with an easy, joking manner that made it seem like he was comfortable with everyone, and everyone was comfortable with him. As much as Charlie wanted to be handing Kara $300 at the end of the weekend, he was pretty sure he was looking at the contest winner right now.

“All right,” Charlie said, writing their brainstorm ideas next to the letter M. “Now the second M stands for Media.” He explained that media was the way that you choose to deliver the message. “Obviously—you’ll be delivering the message face-to-face. But there are different ways to do it—for example … ” He stopped suddenly, looked down at his feet and said, "Good afternoon. What's the scoop?" so quietly they could barely hear him. He looked up again, "Kara, can you show me a better way?"

Grinning impishly, Kara stood up and walked behind the counter. Charlie came up and pretended to be a customer. She smiled, made eye contact and said warmly, "Hey there! What's the scoop?" as if they were best friends that had seen each other the day before. He praised her, trying carefully not to go overboard in front of her friends and had them all take a turn.

Their TAMM chart complete, he sent them all home for the day. Kara collected her purse and then came back to the counter. "Hey, Dad?" she said, kind of shyly. Charlie turned around to face her, smiling at his daughter.

"Yeah, honey?"

"You're doing a really great job," she said and then half-jogged out the door.

Chapter 8

"Hey there!" Charlie said, straightening up behind the counter. "What's the scoop?" He grinned broadly—not just to contribute to the company culture, but because he was so excited to see the customer was his wife.

"How's it going?" she asked. "I came down as soon as I could."

"It's going well," Charlie said. "I was just thinking, I'm here surrounded by all this ice cream all day long, and I don't know how long it's been since I've actually had a cone. Thought you'd like to join me."

"Sure," Andrea said, smiling. She ordered peppermint, and Charlie scooped himself some French silk. They made their way to a booth, and June came out to man the counter while Charlie sat down.

"You seem excited," Andrea said, and Charlie nodded.

"I am," he said. And he had a lot to be excited

about. The festival had been a huge, smashing success. Partway through the first day, Doug had the idea to rethink their use of media to include cell phones. ("Because friends text each other, right?" he had said.) So using the same technique that June had used with the social media site, they had started amassing more and more followers on the page. And then they would send out messages whenever business got slow—like two-for-one deals, or "flavor of the day" deals, or a special deal where you got 10 percent off your order if you brought in your receipt from the day before. Their booth was almost always busy, but, to Charlie's immense surprise, it was June who walked away the top salesperson. Charlie watched her carefully one day—seeing a side of her come out that he had never seen before: friendly, warm and genuine. But there was something else, too, and it took a little while for Charlie to put his finger on it. *She understands the target*, he had realized finally. June, the aspiring musician, knew how to talk to other music lovers, chatting with them about the performances, the instruments and the headliners. People enjoyed Doug and warmed to Kara and the other girls, but they really sought out June.

Excitement about the booth had spread into town, with people coming in after they were done at the festival, or on their way, or if they just needed to sit somewhere with air-conditioning. They ran out of chocolate on the third day, but thankfully Charlie was able to catch Scott and convince him to bring more ice cream on his way through town to his next stop.

On the last day of the festival, a salesman from a local radio station had come in to talk to Charlie about buying some commercials. He had laid out a brochure with several different kinds of media packages—spots following certain programs, several ads a day and even a "celebrity" mention, which meant that the morning radio show team would find a way to work in a discussion about the shop on their show once a week.

Charlie had looked it all over and seriously considered it. Marketing hadn't been something that John really got into—"People want ice cream, they'll buy ice cream!" he had said often, claiming that marketing was all a sham in the end. Charlie wasn't so sure—after all, hadn't the festival been so successful because of all the marketing they had done?

But as soon as he had that thought, Charlie took a moment to pause.

"Wait a minute," he said. "I'm not so sure about this. What station are you from again?"

"89.7, KQGF," the salesman replied.

"Ah," Charlie nodded. "Sports radio."

He turned the salesman down gently, thanked him for his time and walked him to the door. The salesman looked completely confused—but Charlie wasn't sure how to explain to him that it was never going to work. *He has his TAMM backward,* Charlie thought. *He wants to start with media—the radio—and we need to start with the target.* At The Scoop, the target was families with young kids and teenagers. Charlie figured that there were plenty of dads who listened to sports radio—but Charlie also knew that the primary decision maker when it came to ice cream was mom. Buying ad space on an all sports radio station would never have reached his real target audience.

Earlier that morning, Brian had come in, in a very different mood than Charlie had ever seen him. He had recapped the festival's numbers, which were very, very good—and commended Charlie for his innovative use of Internet marketing, but also for the way he had trained the new hires.

"Those kids were actually *excited* to be at work! They really *wanted* to sell ice cream!" Brian had exclaimed.

Charlie had nodded and then cleared his throat. He knew that Brian would not have made a trip to the store just to congratulate him on the festival. "Brian," he started, "I was wondering how your search for the general manager is going." Despite his recent success, Charlie could feel a little bit of his old self resurfacing. He had used the TAMM strategy to try to plan this discussion with Brian—to let him know he was interested in staying on as the permanent GM—but when it came down to it, Charlie was still nervous.

"Well it's going really well," Brian had said, smiling. "In fact, I think I found the guy."

"Oh," Charlie had said, deflating. He had thought that he would have been involved in the process, somehow. He didn't have a plan for what to say in this instance.

"So, what do you think, Charlie?" Brian said. "Do you want to stay on as my general manager here? I don't know anyone else who could have done what you did here this month. This was truly, truly incredible."

So, yes—it had been a good day. He told Andrea all about it and was surprised to see a few tears in her eyes.

"This is good news!" he chided her gently. "Don't cry!"

"I'm sorry," Andrea said, wiping her eyes. "I'm just so proud of you. I know that you were happy at the mill, but I just always felt like … I always felt like there was something more for you, that you could be happier. I'm so glad that you've found it. I haven't seen you like this since high school."

He sent her on her way with promises to bring home more ice cream to celebrate with the girls after supper. "We're all going to gain 50 pounds now that you run the place!" Andrea had laughed, and the laughter was still ringing merrily in Charlie's ears as he set about his office, closing it down for the day.

He heard a stifled cough and shuffling that could only mean that June was getting ready to end her shift. She had thoroughly enjoyed the festival—but since it ended Charlie could tell that something was on her mind. He came out to the front.

"Hey June, could I talk to you?" he asked. He motioned for her to sit at a booth with him. She did, looking a little sullen as she took the earbuds out of her ears.

"I saw Brian was here today," she said before Charlie could speak. "So I guess that you're the general manager for real now?"

"Yes," Charlie said. "I am the general manager for real. And I really have to thank you, June, the festival was such a huge success. It wouldn't have turned out so great without you."

June rolled her eyes, but Charlie thought she was happy with his praise. "Well," Charlie began, about to tell her that he was going to take off for the night if she didn't need anything else, when June suddenly spoke.

"I was really hoping that the festival would be like … I don't know. A networking opportunity for me or something. Something like that. How stupid," she said miserably. She put her hands over her face and sighed. Charlie was stunned. What was he supposed to say to that? June went on.

"I talked to so many people about my music, I even handed out CDs and had stupid business cards with my website on it and everything. I even finally got to talk to one of the local promoters—he came in for ice cream—he loved the mint chocolate chip—and on the third day I finally just told him flat out that he should listen to my music because I was really good. He didn't even take the CD with him when he left." She shook her head. "I'm such an idiot."

Charlie listened silently, feeling terrible for June. What had been a huge leap for her personally had apparently not had the professional return she had been hoping for, and it was exactly the opposite for Charlie. It had all worked out wonderfully for him.

"June, I'm so sorry," he said. "I don't know

anything about music—but I wish there was something to do to help."

"I just—I wish—" June said and then looked up at him. "I wish I knew a way to talk to people, you know, to get them to do what I want."

Charlie sat in surprised silence. June continued, "You know—I feel like if I hadn't gotten so nervous and tongue-tied, if I just knew what to say."

"June," Charlie started, smiling and reaching for a napkin and his pen. "You're not going to believe this, but this is something I can actually help with."

"Really?" she asked him, sitting up quickly.

"Absolutely," Charlie said, drawing on the napkin, which he then pushed across the table to her.

She looked down at it, frowning, and then looked back up and said, "TAMM? What's that?"

"Target, action, message, media," he said. "And that's how we're going to get you on that stage next year."

TAMM®

TARGET»ACTION»MESSAGE»MEDIA

Chapter 9

Remember the last time you said something that you regretted? If you're anything like me, you spent the rest of the day asking yourself "what was I thinking?" Sometimes our mouth gets out ahead of our brain, and we say things before we've thought them through. It makes for bad communication, obviously, and we often pay for our indiscretion with an apology later.

Weak marketing happens the same way. We get so excited about coming up with a message that we do the job out of order. As we saw in Charlie's story, a Message that doesn't account for the Target audience can be a complete waste of time and energy (advertising to high school students in the newspaper?). Failing to consider the desired Action can also weaken your brand message (the difference between "I want customers to buy ice cream" and "I want customers to tell their friends they just had the best ice cream ever").

You just can't get ahead of yourself when it

comes to the TAMM method. First comes the Target, then comes the Action, then comes the Message. You address Media last. You can't address the steps out of order or you weaken your communication.

One of our clients is a large Midwestern distributor of electrical, plumbing and HVAC parts. When an electrician needs a dozen light switches to finish a house, he calls our client. They sell millions of parts every year, and most of them are to contractors. They never sell to end users (like homeowners, for example). They are a classic business-to-business wholesaler, and they have been for more than a century.

One of the very first challenges we experienced when we started working with this client was a general confusion about their Target audience. We would be gathering information for a sales piece for plumbers, for example, and the manufacturer would send us a product description that said "the comfort of the Flushomatic 1,000 is unsurpassed" or something like that.

If you're not thinking strategically, that product benefit sounds perfectly reasonable. After all, who doesn't like a comfortable toilet? But once you apply the TAMM method, things look different. Remember, our client never sells to homeowners. They sell to plumbers, and plumbers are never going to use the Flushomatic 1,000—they're going to sell and install the Flushomatic 1,000. That means they aren't interested in comfort, at least not directly.

Instead, they're interested in an entirely different set of benefits: How long does it take to install? How many tools do I need to install it? How much can I mark it up before I sell it? If plumbers are interested in things like comfort and attractiveness, it's only because those characteristics may help them to sell the toilet.

So instead of having "the comfort of the Flushomatic 1,000 is unsurpassed" in our sales piece, we include a benefit like "the Flushomatic 1,000 installs in just 10 minutes, so you can fit more service calls into your day."

The Action step can be confusing too. We work with a large insurance company that covers everything from huge corporations to mom-and-pop businesses. When we first started working for this client, we learned right away that they do very little "personal lines" insurance, that is, life, health and auto. So we identified our Target as business decision makers—in particular, those who got a vote on choosing an insurance policy.

When it came to the Action step, the obvious answer to the question "What do we want the target to do?" was "switch their insurance to our client."

This is the obvious answer but not the correct answer. Have you ever changed your insurance? It's a headache, to say the least. Think about how much paperwork it took. Now pretend you're a business with 500 employees; take that paperwork and multiply it times 1,000. Making the decision to change insurance carriers is a massive undertaking that inevitably involves a lot of people. That's a lot to ask of someone after they've simply seen your website or TV commercial.

Instead, what if we defined our Action as something much more attainable—and less overwhelming to the Target. How about something like "We want the Target to give us an appointment for a free audit of their coverage needs." That's a lot less ambitious, but also a lot more realistic. Besides, it's not likely that any marketing message could completely change someone's mind about something as important as insurance anyway. But it might convince them to make a relatively painless decision like agreeing to meet with someone with new ideas.

In fact, unless you are promoting a retail offer (Sale! Everything must go!), realistic Action goals tend to be fairly subtle, especially when you are working to impact the overall perception of your brand. Jack Trout and Al Ries famously said that positioning is a battle for the mind of the consumer. So your Action may be a change in perception rather than an actual, physical deed. For example, you may define the action that you want your Target audience to take like this: "To recognize our brand's warranty as the industry's best."

That's a realistic Action goal. Once the product is differentiated (another famous Trout quote: "Differentiate or die!") as having the industry's best warranty coverage, it's up to the other parts of your marketing mix—and the sales team—to finish the job by providing positive touchpoints and closing the deal.

Now that you've decided on the who and the why, it's time to come up with the how. That's where your Message and your Media come in.

Ahh, the Message. This is the sexy part of marketing. This is what they make movies and TV shows about. No director has ever cried, "Cut! We need to show them talking about the Target audience and the Action that we want that Target audience to take." Instead, they focus on wild brainstorming sessions filled with unbridled creativity and brilliant ideas about the Message.

Is it really like that in a marketing agency? It is, sometimes, and I'm grateful for that. Wild brainstorming sessions are a lot of fun. *But they can also be pretty expensive if you don't already have a handle on the first two letters in TAMM.* So we require something called a Creative Brief before each and every brainstorm. It spells out the Target and the Action and makes the account team (an agency's salespeople) put them in writing for everyone who is attending the brainstorm. That way everybody can suggest strategically sound Message ideas during the brainstorming session itself.

We work with a bank, and one of our first jobs was to create a positioning statement for them. Much more than just a slogan, we needed a phrase that solidified the bank's brand in the mind of their Target audience. This simple statement would accompany the bank logo at all times. We knew that the Target was a combination of rural customers (where the bank got its start) and metropolitan customers (where the bank had recently opened a branch). More specifically, we identified that their most likely potential customers were adults who valued the "hometown service" they had grown up with.

A secondary Target was the bank's own internal staff. They had never had a slogan or positioning statement, but they were proud of their logo, which featured a majestic tree. The Message needed to take that into account, since the positioning statement would be used in conjunction with the bank's logo.

When we considered the action that we wanted the Target audience to take, we knew that it was important for them to see the bank as a part of their own story—filled with employees that treated them like old friends. In fact, our proposed creative treatment for print ads and television commercials prominently featured employees with a caption revealing their hometown. The main Action goal for the positioning statement (and for the initial advertising campaign) was for "the Target audience to perceive the bank and its employees in the same way that they remember a trusted friend with a shared background."

At the same time, the nation was in the midst of a massive financial crisis, and some of the bank's management wanted to make sure that we didn't position the bank as "small," because they felt that potential customers might misconstrue that as "weak." So the secondary Action that we needed people to take when they saw the positioning statement was something like "associate the bank's brand with strength and security."

We considered the Target audience and the Action, and they led us to a unique message that now accompanies the bank's tree-based logo everywhere it is displayed: "Our roots make us stronger." It has become an integral part of the bank's identity and a foundation on which much of their marketing and communication is based. In fact, a long-running billboard features a die-cut tree protruding high above the top of the sign with a simple headline: the positioning statement itself.

Media is represented by the last letter in TAMM, but that doesn't mean it is any less important. Consider that the world's most effective, strategically planned Message is wasted if it is delivered to the wrong audience. That's what choosing the wrong Media will do. It will deliver your message to people who just aren't interested in your product or service. Talk about a waste of resources.

Have you ever wondered why you seem to see or hear the same commercial all the time, no matter where you are or what you are watching? For example, a new movie is coming out that you are interested in, and it seems like its promotional Messages are everywhere. Well, you're wrong. Those Messages aren't everywhere. *They're just everywhere you are.* That's because you've been identified as the Target audience, and a savvy media planner has done her homework, then scheduled the Message to be delivered by the Media that you are most likely to listen to. If you are a middle-aged man that enjoys hunting and fishing, switch over to a TV channel that your wife watches, and you will see a completely different set of advertisers. The more segmentation we experience in our media, the more pronounced this becomes.

Let's go back to our longtime client that sells commercial insurance. Their Target audience is mainly upper management in businesses of all sizes. As you can well imagine, CEOs and COOs are busy individuals. They might be men, and they might be women. They certainly have money but not a lot of free time. The old-school way of thinking was to reach these folks through traditional, mainstream media. This isn't completely wrong—after all, it's possible that the CEO of a hospital will watch the season finale of a popular TV show—but it is also the definition of overkill. If we buy a commercial on a popular TV program, we are paying for all of the viewers, even though the number of potential customers (CEOs, COOs, etc.) who are watching is very, very small. It's like killing mosquitoes with a sledgehammer.

It's much more cost effective to find a Medium that lets you get in front of more of your Target audience without all the waste. In our part of the country, the answer is sports. Successful companies have suites at popular college hockey and football venues, and colleges treat their successful alumni like royalty, so they tend to show up for games. That means more potential insurance decision makers per impression (i.e., more CEOs per viewer) for a sports sponsorship in an arena ("This goal brought to you by … ") than for an episode of a hit TV show.

A TAMM breakdown looks something like this: Target—upper management in businesses; Action—allow the client to speak to them about their insurance; Message—"We understand you and your business. In fact, we support the same causes you do, such as this sports team"; Media—sports venue sponsorships for scoreboards, video screens and hockey dasher boards. This strategy has been very successful for this client, and we've been able to stick with it for many years because of its cost effectiveness.

Lest you get the impression that we aren't fans of technology, let me give you a few examples of how we've put the TAMM strategy into action online. One of our national clients sells wild bird food. Their primary Target is female homeowners over the age of 40. The Action we agreed upon is to encourage the Target audience to consider these birds as their "outdoor pets" and consequently, to believe that they are worth feeding our premium wild bird food. The Message is to "Attract The Extraordinary," and the Media we are using is a combination of a website designed specifically with women (and mobile devices) in mind, along with a strong, active presence on Facebook. Women of this age love Facebook as a way of sharing with their family and friends, and we've positioned their wild bird feeding as part of their gardening, landscaping and outdoor living experience. It also gives our client an easy way to deliver information about promotions and even the occasional coupon.

We've also had tremendous success with pay-per-click advertising for many of our clients. One of them hosts an online auction for salvaged recreational vehicles and boats. The Target is men who want to save money over buying a new vehicle and don't consider the idea of doing some repair work to be a deal breaker. The Action we focus on is getting them to start watching an auction on the site, hopefully creating an account at the same time. Since not everyone knows that salvage auctions—particularly online salvage auctions—exist, the Message is informative: "Save even more than buying used by buying salvage!" The Media we chose is Google, the world's most popular search engine. People searching for "used boats," for example, are a perfect fit. To give you an idea of how beneficial it is to think hard about every aspect of TAMM—including Media—we've also found that Bing, the second most popular search engine in the United States, performs especially well for campers and RVs. This shouldn't be a surprise when you consider that Bing used to be called MSN (Microsoft Network), one of the original search engines and a home page favorite for older users. Older Web users = great audience for recreational vehicles.

In other words, any communication, whether it is online or offline, benefits from a TAMM session. In fact, strategic thinking is even more important in the constantly evolving landscape of the Internet and mobile Web. It's easy to miss the mark because your marks are always on the move. TAMM ensures that you don't waste your time or money chasing the wrong Target audience, asking for the wrong Action (We want them to click, but where should they go then? Two words: landing pages.), missing a chance to customize your Message to a very specific audience or choosing an outdated Media outlet.

The TAMM process is part of our culture here. We use it for virtually every decision we make. I'm still amazed at how a little strategic thinking can illuminate fallacies in our way of thinking or misguided assumptions about Target audiences. Even

I catch myself chasing the wrong Target audience or looking for the wrong Action now and then. But a short TAMM session gets me back on track before I've gone too far.

What should you use TAMM for? Try using it before your next brainstorm. Use it before you get involved with a marketing project like a commercial or a newspaper ad. Do a TAMM overview of your website—you might be surprised at the results. The truth is that a TAMM session—whether you do it solo or with others—will improve any and all of your communication, from press releases to sales calls. There is never a bad time to think strategically about your next move.

But you must follow through. Thomas Edison once said "Vision without execution is hallucination." Use TAMM to analyze and think strategically about your communication, then put your ideas to work and measure the results to ensure that you get real results. If not, have another TAMM session to learn what you missed the first time. You'll never have to ask yourself "What was I thinking?" again.

We have a simple matrix that we use here that helps us to organize the TAMM process. I've included a diagram of it here. Feel free to make copies or make your own version (it works well in a spreadsheet program). It can be a helpful tool when you are going though each of the TAMM steps. Just write your ideas in the respective blanks, and you can see how everything fits together.

I hope you liked Charlie's story. More importantly, I hope you adopt the TAMM process in your own business. I am positive that it will help you to shape good decisions when it comes to your communication.

TAMM
TARGET»ACTION»MESSAGE»MEDIA

T.A.M.M. Strategy

Target(s)	Action	Message	Media		
Who?	Why?	How?	What?	When?	How Much?

Sources

Ries, A. & Trout, J. (2000) *Positioning: The Battle for Your Mind.* McGraw-Hill.

Trout, J. & Revkin, S. (2001) *Differentiate or Die: Survival in Our Era of Killer Competition.* Wiley.

About The Author

Steve Eickman is the president of Anchor Marketing, a brand-building agency with offices in Grand Forks, North Dakota, and Phoenix, Arizona. He has been successfully building and positioning brands for clients for more than 25 years. He also works as a consultant for up-and-coming businesses in Northwestern Minnesota.

Steve lives on a lake and enjoys fishing, working on classic cars and spending time with his wife, sons and grandchildren. He is available for speaking engagements. Contact him via www.anchorwebsite.com.